THE XXL Baking Recipe Book

Quick and Delicious Baking Secrets for Family and Friends incl. Cakes, Bread, Cookies, Pies, and More

Sarah Berry

TABLE OF CONTENTS

Introduction

Throughout this book, our intention is to show you some of the secrets involved in great baking. While others maintain that the secret ingredient is love, we know that great baking starts with a great recipe. To give you the best possible chances at creating a culinary masterpiece, we have collected some of the quickest, tastiest, and most cherished baking recipes from throughout the land.

As well as containing recipes that will inject some sparkle into your baked goods, we have collated some top baking tips, straight from the mouths of the chefs themselves. So sit back, relax, and turn your tastebud settings to "tingling." It is time we got down to business... The business of baking.

Baking Vs Cooking: What is the Difference?

Baking is a specific form of cooking. While all baking is cooking, not all cooking is baking. The main difference that separates the two, is the use of the oven.

When we bake goods, we cook them in the oven from start to finish. When we cook, we use a variety of techniques to achieve an edible delight. We can cook everything from sauces to ice cream – but we can only bake if that cooking is performed in the oven.

Baking Vs Roasting: What is the Difference?

Interestingly, and just to confuse you further, not everything baked in an oven from start to finish is thought of as "baked goods." For example, a whole chicken or beef joint cooked in the oven from start to finish would be known as a "roast" dish. This is because we don't refer to meats or vegetables as being baked goods. Why? It is just a colloquialism. We would call meats or vegetables cooked in an oven "roasted" as opposed to "baked."

It is this distinction between being baked or being roasted that conjures two different dishes to mind. If you tell someone you will bring baked goods to the party, they assume you will bring cakes or breads. If you tell someone you will bring a roast to the party, they assume you will bring a roasted meat dish, with or without vegetables.

What Key Elements Make Baking successful?

There are many factors which come together to create a perfect baked dish. The oven temperature, the length of time the dish gets cooked for, and the recipe, are the three most crucial factors. However, other things can make or break a good dish too. Things like beating instead of whisking, folding instead of beating, and sieving your floor to make it extra fine, all come into play.

Let's review some of these factors before we move on.

Oven Temperature

The temperature of your oven drastically affects how your baked goods will turn out. Too high and the food will be undercooked in the centre and charred on the outside. Too low and the food might not be fully cooked.

As a guide: denser foods take longer to cook than foods that are light and airy. A cake might take 20-25 minutes while a bread, whose dough is denser, might take 25-35 minutes, even though they are of comparable size.

A Preheated Oven

An oven which is preheated is cooking your baked goods at exactly the right temperature from the start. When we put food in a cold oven, the food must then pass through all the temperatures up until the correct one. Variations in temperature like this might affect the quality and integrity of the food. If you want perfect, consistent, baked goods, then the same temperature every time is the desired standard.

Length of Time Baked

If you bake your food for too long, it will become tough and carbonated (burned). Bake something in the oven for too little time, on the other hand, and it may still be raw on the inside.

Additionally, you should never open your oven to check on food before the prescribed time has passed. Each second the oven door is open loses 10C//50F of your temperature. As we know, temperature fluctuations affect both cooking times and the quality of our baking. Resist the urge to check.

Recipe

You cannot underestimate the importance of following your recipe. Good baking requires good powers of observation. Following the recipe to the letter means preheating your oven, using the correct amounts of each ingredient, baking at the correct temperature and for the correct timespan, and any other intricacies needed to bake perfect foods.

If you have followed your recipe properly, you will end up with the same appearance, texture, and flavour of food, every time you cook it. The recipe sets the quality standard of your food. How well you follow it will irrevocably impact the quality of baking you end up with.

Top Tips for Baking Success

We can't send you off into the world of bakery without giving you some sound advice on how to be a successful baker. Before you pick up the apron and begin, here are some top tips that professional bakers swear by.

Place cakes in the centre of your oven

Unless the recipe states otherwise, bake everything in the centre of your oven. Be sure there is room for air to move around the food in all directions. This is how a traditional oven heats the food evenly.

Get the weights spot on

Weights and measurements are too important to be given in cups. The size of a cup differs in every household. Stick to g//oz and try to be as precise as possible.

Make adjustments as per the recipe

Where a recipe says "beat" instead of "whisk," follow these instructions. Adjust temperatures too, soft butter, cold butter, or melted butter, can make a significant difference to the recipe. Cooking is chemistry at its heart. Be precise.

Invest in baking parchment and ring moulds

Ring moulds are used for everything from cheesecakes to parmesan crisps. Invest in a set of four if you want to impress your friends and family with baked dessert delights. Parchment paper is your best friend for stopping cakes, breads, biscuits, and cookies from sticking to your baking tins.

Chill cookie dough, warm bread doughs

As a rule of thumb, cookie doughs which are cooled and left to chill for an hour or two, create fluffy, light cookies. When left to heat and go mushy, the cookies are denser and flatter.

Contrarily, a warm bread dough allows the yeast to ferment. You will have a light, fluffy bread. A cold bread dough means the yeast is no longer working. If it gets cooled too soon, the yeast will not ferment and your bread will be flat.

Confectioners' sugar or icing sugar?

Depending on where you live, you may substitute icing sugar for confectioner's sugar and vice versa. To make icing sugar from normal sugar, place caster sugar into a food processor and blend it well. Powdered sugar is just sugar blended into smaller particles than what you would find in caster sugar. Again, caster sugar is simply granulated sugar blended into smaller particles.

Check your substitutions

If you need to substitute an ingredient, be sure to have cooked the recipe at least once beforehand. There are some recipes that can have ingredients switched out easily. For example, if you wanted to make a vegetarian shepherd's pie, switching out the lamb mince for soy mince or Quorn could be a healthy alternative.

Separating eggs

To separate an egg white from an egg yolk, crack the egg open over a bowl. Pour the yolk into one half of the shell, then back into the other half of the shell. Let the white fall out and focus on the yolk. You can use your fingers instead of the yolk, but a professional baker would try not to touch the eggs if they could help it.

Advice on yeast

In general, a recipe for bread will require yeast. The recipe will state which kind of yeast, as it may need dried, active, or fresh yeast. Yeast is activated by adding lukewarm water and sugar (which it eats) and placing in a warm place for 10-15 minutes. Salt deactivates yeast over time. If you are baking bread, try to add the sugar at the beginning and the salt towards the end.

Yeast should always be kept warm, but not hot. Do not pour boiling water straight over your yeast as it may kill it. Instant yeast can be added straight to your recipe without activation. Just keep it away from the salt.

Cooling advice

If you don't have a wire cooling rack, you can cool baked goods using the inside of your grill pan. Be sure your grill is off at the time! Try not to remove cakes and loaves from their tins until the baked goods are properly cooled. To remove them before proper cooling increases the chances that they will break apart. Cutting bread before it is properly cooled is also a bad idea since it will still be cooking for a while after it comes out of the oven. Leave loaves to cool for 15-20 minutes for a warmed, but cooked, loaf.

Checking on baked goods

If you are waiting for a cake to rise and want to check if it is ready or not, inserting a toothpick into the mixture (or a butter knife) in the thickest part will tell you. If the toothpick draws out clean, the food is cooked. If it is still doughy, the mixture needs more time.

Bicarbonate of Soda Vs Baking Powder?

Both ingredients can produce bubbles within your mixture, allowing more air to get inside your baked goods. Bicarbonate of soda requires another acidic ingredient plus liquid to be activated. Baking powder is bicarbonate of soda which has had cream of tartare added into it. This means it does not need an acid to activate, it only needs liquid. Both will produce a light, bubbly texture that keeps baked goods aeriated.

Whether you require baking powder or bicarbonate of soda will depend on the other ingredients. Follow the recipe for best results. As an added aside, many American recipe books stick to baking powder or baking soda, while many British recipes call for bicarbonate of soda. Recipes in Britain from before the 1990s would often call for both bicarbonate of soda and cream of tartare. This can still be found nowadays in old cookbooks.

What Baking Equipment Do I Need?

To start baking at home, you will need some basic pieces of equipment.

Basic Baking Equipment:
- A large bowl, preferably metal
- A whisk
- A wooden spoon
- A spatula
- A fork
- An oven
- A cake tin or baking tray
- Scales, digital or otherwise
- Sieve

As your hobby progresses, you may wish to invest in other baking equipment. We would recommend some of the following.

Optional Baking Equipment:
- An electronic mixer
- An electric whisk
- Parchment paper
- Ring moulds
- A loaf tin
- A muffin tin
- A cooling rack (you can use your grill pan tray)
- Reusable pastry bag and nozzles
- Measuring cups and spoons
- Cookie cutters

- Oven thermometer
- A bench scraper

There are plenty of other optional pieces of baking equipment but if you have all the above, you are well on your way to baking success.

A Glossary of Baking Terms

There are those of us who are complete beginners and we welcome each one of you. However, you need to get up to speed on bakery terms before we go any further. We have outlined the key baking terms below as a reference point for the rest of the book. If you come across a term in a recipe that you do not recognise, you will find it here.

Whisking

When we "whisk" our food we use a specific device to do so, which is known as a whisk. This device can be motorized to make our lives easier. An electric whisk will take egg whites to meringue mix in less than 5 minutes. By hand, whisking egg whites into meringue takes up to three times as long.

As a pro tip: whip cream by whisking it in a metal bowl. Whisking in a metal bowl generates extra friction which will help get the job done faster. This works for anything you need to whisk until stiffened.

Beating

When beating a mixture, you are required to use a metal spoon or fork. Contrarily, beating can mean whisking in some circumstances. The recipe should make this clear. The purpose of beating with a metal spoon or fork is to get air into a mixture that cannot be whisked to stiff peaks.

Folding

We usually "fold" flour into a pre-whisked mixture of other ingredients. Folding is done with a spatula or metal spoon. We run the spatula around the outside of the bowl and fold it on top of itself into the centre. We repeat this until the flour is gone. When we fold, we usually sieve the flour or icing sugar. The purpose of folding is to stop the air from leaving the mixture as we add the heavier flour.

Kneading

We use the term "kneading" to describe the act of working a dough mixture. Typically used in the baking of breads, kneading the dough means to stretch, press, and distort the mixture.

We knead the bread to encourage the formation of gluten strands within a dough mixture. These form when liquid is added to some flour. The more you stretch and work your dough, the stronger these strands will be. This leads to a denser bread, so be careful not to over-knead.

Lining

When we say "lining" in bakery, we mean creating a layer between the baked goods and the tray or tin we are using to cook it. The easiest way to line a tin is with baking parchment, although dessert, cake, and bread tins, are often lined with butter and a dusting of flour. We would "grease" a tin with butter or non-stick spray to help the parchment paper stick.

Proofing

When baking breads, we often leave the dough to rise in a technique called "proofing." Proofing allows the yeast in your dough to do its job of making the mixture rise. It rises because the yeast expels carbon dioxide as it grows. This is a fermentation process which makes a better bread.

Sieving

A Sieve is a piece of kitchen equipment which is used to finely sieve your dry ingredients. It keeps flour particles separated, allowing more air to get into your mixture. We use sieving during baking cakes and desserts which need plenty of air in the mixture so that they are bouncy and light instead of dense.

Creaming

When creaming two baking ingredients together, you are blending them until they form a cream-like consistency. We use this term when referring to blending butter and sugar together, as we do to form a basic blend for many cake recipes.

Rubbing

When we "rub-in" a substance in baking, we use one of two techniques. We use the fingers of our hands and avoid the mixture touching the palms. The aim of rubbing ingredients into one another is to achieve a breadcrumb-like consistency. We usually rub butter into flour to make this texture. It allows as much air into the mixture as possible, while ensuring the two ingredients are well blended. We do not want to melt the butter, which is why we avoid using the palms of our hands.

The two ways to rub-in ingredients are as follows:

a) Pick up a scoop of mixture using only your fingers. This is best done from above, as if your fingers are a crane closing. Hold one hand flat and drop the scoop onto its fingers using the scooped hand. Holding your flat hand facing away from you, flatten your scoop hand and push the material away from your body to the side. This causes friction which rubs the two ingredients together.

b) Using each hand as a scoop, pick up a little material at a time and rub your thumb across your forefingers. Slowly let the material fall through those fingers as you do so.

Remember: if your palms have flour on them, you are not rubbing-in correctly.

Conversion Tables

Where needed, conversions throughout this recipe book will be given in UK//US (ca).

°C	°F	Fan Oven	Gas Mark
170	325	150	3
180	350	160	4
190	375	170	5
200	400	180	6
220	425	200	7
230	450	210	8

Millilitres	Fl Ounces
1ml	0.04
5ml	0.18
10ml	0.35
50ml	1.76
100ml	17.6
1000ml	170.6

Grams	Ounces
1g	0.0353oz
5g	0.1764oz
10g	0.3527oz
50g	1.7637oz
100g	3.5274oz
1000g	35.2740oz

Recipes

Baked Breads

Simple White Loaf

MAKES 10-12 SLICES
PREP TIME: 2 HRS 20 MINS | COOK TIME: 25 MINS | TOTAL TIME: 2 HRS 55 MINS
NET CARBS PER SLICE: 38G//1.3OZ | PROTEIN: 6G//0.2OZ |
FAT: 4G//0.14OZ | FIBER: 2G//0.07OZ | KCAL: 200

INGREDIENTS

- 500g//17.6oz strong white bread flour
- 7g//0.2oz instant yeast
- 300ml//10.1floz of lukewarm water
- 2 tbsp olive oil
- 1.5 tsp salt
- Self-raising flour for dusting

INSTRUCTIONS

1 Mix bread flour and yeast into a large bowl.

2 Make a well in the middle of the mixture, then gradually pour the water and the olive oil into it.

3 Mix with a knife until the mixture becomes a dough. It should be wet enough to remove all material from the sides of the bowl, but stiff enough that you can knead it.

4   Once the dough has come together, sprinkle in the salt to deactivate the yeast.

5   Turn the dough out onto a floured surface and knead for ten minutes.

6   Place your dough back inside the bowl and cover it loosely with clingfilm. Leave to rise somewhere warm (but not hot) for 2 hours or more.

7   When ready to bake your bread, preheat your oven to 220C//428F//gas mark 7.

8   The dough will now be much larger than it was when you left it. Remove it from the bowl and place it on a floured surface. Fold it in on itself twice. Do not fully knead it.

9   Place the dough into a lined loaf tin. If you do not have a bread tin, the dough can be shaped into a ball and placed on a baking tray. Score the surface of the bread with a knife.

10   Place inside the oven and cook for 25 minutes or until the bread has turned golden brown.

11   Do not cut your bread until it has cooled slightly as it will still be cooking in the middle.

Wholesome Wholemeal Bread

MAKES 10-12 SLICES
PREP TIME: 2HRS 20 MINS | COOK TIME: 25 MINS | TOTAL TIME: 2HRS 55 MINS
NET CARBS PER SLICE: 23.64G//0.8OZ | PROTEIN: 3.86G//0.13OZ |
FAT: 2.48G// 0.08OZ | FIBER: 2.8G//0.09OZ | KCAL: 128

INGREDIENTS

- ○ 400g//14.1oz strong wholemeal bread flour
- ○ A pinch of salt
- ○ A pinch of sugar
- ○ 7g//0.24oz instant yeast sachet
- ○ 300ml//10.1floz lukewarm water
- ○ 2 tablespoons olive oil
- ○ Wholemeal flour for dusting

INSTRUCTIONS

1 Mix your wholemeal flour, the sugar, the salt, and the instant yeast together in a bowl.

2 Create a well in the centre, then gradually add the water and the oil to the well.

3 Mix the water into the dough using a knife. Once it is coming away from the sides of the bowl freely you can stop adding water. The mixture should come together into a ball without being sticky.

4 Turn your dough onto a floured surface and knead for 10 minutes.

5 Cover with clingfilm and place somewhere warm (but not hot) for 2 hours or more. The dough will proof and rise.

6 Preheat the oven to 200C//392F//gas mark 6.

7 Remove the dough from the bowl and place it on a floured surface. Turn it over on itself twice.

8 Place the dough into a lined loaf tin or form into a ball and place on a lined baking tray. Score the top of the loaf with a knife.

9 Place inside the oven and cook for 30-35 minutes or until the crust is golden.

10 Allow your bread to cool a little before you cut it as it will still be cooking on the inside.

Sourdough Bread

MAKES 10-12 SLICES
PREP TIME: 8 DAYS 12 HRS 15 MINS | COOK TIME: 30 MINS |
TOTAL TIME: 8 DAYS 12 HRS 55 MINS

NET CARBS PER SLICE: 50G//1.7OZ | PROTEIN: 8G//0.28OZ |
FIBER: 2G//0.07OZ | FAT: 0.9G//0.03OZ | KCAL: 240

INGREDIENTS (STARTER)

- ◯ 700g//24.7oz strong white bread flour
- ◯ Warm water

INGREDIENTS (BREAD)

- ◯ 500g//17.63oz strong white bread flour plus extra for dusting
- ◯ 1 tsp salt
- ◯ 1 tsp sugar
- ◯ 300g//10.58oz sourdough starter
- ◯ 250ml//8.4floz lukewarm water
- ◯ 1 tbsp rapeseed oil

INSTRUCTIONS

1 Place 100g flour and 150 ml of water in a sealable jar and mix well. Leave the jar open for half an hour and then seal it. Place it somewhere warm but not hot.

2 For 6 consecutive days, add an extra 100g flour and 150ml water per day. By day 7 your starter will be usable.

3 You can keep your sourdough starter in the fridge for as long as you need it. You will have to feed more flour and water into the mixture every 4 days to keep the yeast alive.

4 To make your sourdough bread, place all the dry ingredients in a bowl and mix well.

5 Make a well in the middle and pour the sourdough starter and the water into it. Keep the remaining portion of your starter for another loaf and remember to feed it fresh flour over the coming days.

6 Mix the dough together with a knife until it comes freely away from the sides of the bowl into a ball.

7 Turn the ball out onto a floured surface and knead it well for ten minutes. When it is ready, it should have a soft, stretchy texture.

8 Take a clean bowl and line it with oil, then put your dough inside it and cover it with clingfilm. Leave it to proof for 3-4 hrs.

9 Remove it from this bowl and place it into a clean bowl, this time cover it loosely. Leave it to rise overnight. Sourdough takes two-three times longer to rise than any other dough.

10 Top tip: the longer you leave a sourdough to rise for, the better the flavour. When it is ready it will have doubled in size and will have a few air bubbles.

11 Preheat your oven to 230C//446F//gas mark 8 and line a baking tray with parchment paper or prepare a loaf tin.

12 Place an ovenproof dish containing water in the bottom shelf of the oven to create steam.

13 Put the dough onto your tray and score it with a knife. Place the dough in the oven and bake for 30-40 minutes.

14 Remove from the oven and cool for 20 minutes before cutting, as the bread will still be cooking on the inside.

Poppy Seed Rolls

MAKES 8 ROLLS
PREP TIME: 30 MINS PLUS 3 HRS PROVING |
COOK TIME: 20 MINS | TOTAL TIME: 3 HRS 50 MINS

NET CARBS PER ROLL: 48G/1.7OZ | PROTEIN: 9G//0.31OZ |
FIBER: 2.6G//0.09OZ | FAT: 7G//0.03OZ | KCAL: 255

INGREDIENTS

- ○ 500g//17.63oz strong white bread flour
- ○ 1 tsp salt
- ○ 1 tsp granulated sugar
- ○ 7g//0.25oz fast action yeast
- ○ 30g//1oz butter, softened
- ○ 75ml//2.5floz lukewarm milk
- ○ 1 tbsp cold milk
- ○ 2 tbsp roasted poppy seeds

INSTRUCTIONS

1	Mix the flour, salt, sugar, and yeast together in a bowl.

2	Rub in the butter until it has a breadcrumb consistency.

3	Add in the warm milk and combine into a dough.

4   Turn the dough onto a lightly floured surface and knead for ten minutes or until it is smooth.

5   Put the dough back into the bowl, cover it, and allow it to rise in a warm place. Within an hour it should double in size.

6   Remove the dough from the bowl and preheat the oven to 220C//428F// gas mark 6.

7   Knock the air out of the dough by turning it over on itself a few times. Do not overwork it.

8   Separate your dough into 8 portions and place them on a lined baking tray.

9   Brush them with the tbsp of cold milk and sprinkle them with the poppy seeds.

10 Bake for 15-20 minutes or until golden brown.

11 Remove from the oven and leave to cool for at least 15 minutes before serving.

Sweet Breads

Banana Bread Recipe

MAKES 8-10 SLICES

PREP TIME: 15 MINS | COOK TIME: 45 MINS | TOTAL TIME: 1 HR

NET CARBS PER 2 SLICES: 53G//1.86OZ | PROTEIN: 5G//0.17OZ |
FIBER: 2G//0.07OZ | FAT: 11G//0.38OZ | KCAL: 334

INGREDIENTS

- ○ 285g//10oz self raising flour
- ○ A pinch of salt
- ○ 110g//4oz butter, softened
- ○ 225g//8oz caster sugar
- ○ 2 overripe bananas
- ○ 2 drops vanilla essence
- ○ 2 large eggs

INSTRUCTIONS

1 Preheat oven to 180C//356F//gas mark 4.

2 Take a small bowl and sieve your flour into it. Add the salt and mix it well, then set it aside.

3 Place the butter and the sugar in a large bowl and cream them together with a wooden spoon.

4   On a separate plate, mash the bananas until they are gooey and sticky, then add them to the creamed butter and sugar.

5   Next, add the vanilla essence, then take a metal fork and beat the eggs into the wet mixture. The object is to get as much air into the mixture as possible without whisking it.

6   Add a little flour at a time to the mixture and fold it in using a spatula or metal spoon.

7   Line a cake or loaf tin with parchment paper and spoon the mixture into it.

8   Place in the oven and cook for 45 minutes or until the top has turned golden brown.

9   Remove from the oven and leave to cool for at least 20 minutes before serving as it will be extremely hot.

Simple Sweet Baps

MAKES 8 PORTIONS
PREP TIME: 1 HR MINS | COOK TIME: 20 MINS | TOTAL TIME: 1HR 20 MINS

NET CARBS PER 30G BAP: 16G//0.56OZ | PROTEIN: 3G//0.105OZ | FIBER: 0.9G//0.03OZ | FAT: 2.2G//0.07OZ | KCAL: 96

INGREDIENTS

- ⭕ 1 7g//0.05oz packet of dried yeast
- ⭕ 110ml//3.71floz of warm water
- ⭕ 1 tbsp sugar
- ⭕ A pinch of salt
- ⭕ 250g//8.18oz plain flour
- ⭕ one large egg, beaten
- ⭕ 25g//0.88oz of softened butter
- ⭕ 2 tbsp strawberry jam
- ⭕ 100g//3.50oz mixed fruit

INSTRUCTIONS

1 Mix the yeast and the warm water together with the sugar and stir well. Cover with clingfilm and leave in a warm place for 10 minutes. When it turns frothy it is ready to use.

2 Mix the salt and flour together in a separate large bowl. Make a well in the centre and add in your yeast mix. Add half of the egg and the butter and mix it together into a dough.

3 Knead the dough for ten minutes or until smooth.

4 Return the dough to the bowl, cover it loosely, and set it back in the warm place to rise for 20 minutes.

5 Preheat the oven to 200C//392F//gas mark 6.

6 Remove the dough from the bowl and push the air out of it. Divide it into 8 balls. Roll each of the 8 balls flat on a floured surface.

7 Smear the flattened dough with jam and fill with a little mixed fruit, then pinch the balls closed.

8 Put in the oven for 20 minutes or until golden brown. Leave to cool for 15 minutes or more, the contents will be hot.

Cinnamon Rolls

MAKES 12 ROLLS
PREP TIME: 1HR 45MINS (INCLUDING PROOFING TIME) |
COOK TIME: 30 MINS | TOTAL TIME: 2 HRS 15 MINS
NET CARBS PER 88G ROLL: 47G//1.65OZ | PROTEIN: 3.8G//0.13OZ |
FIBER: 1.2G//0.04OZ | FAT: 9.9G//0.349OZ | KCAL: 290

INGREDIENTS

- ○ 350g//12.34oz plain flour
- ○ 7g//0.24oz sachet dried instant yeast
- ○ 2 tbsp cinnamon
- ○ 100g//3.52oz granulated sugar
- ○ A pinch of salt
- ○ 40g//1.41oz butter
- ○ 70ml//2.36floz cold water
- ○ 120ml//4.05floz whole milk
- ○ 2 drops vanilla essence
- ○ I large egg, beaten
- ○ 120g//4.23oz icing sugar

INSTRUCTIONS

1. In a large bowl, add the plain flour to the dried instant yeast. Mix in 1 tbsp of cinnamon, half the sugar, and the salt. Set it aside for later.

2. Melt half the butter in a saucepan over a low heat. Add in the water, the milk, the vanilla essence and lastly the egg. The mixture should be no more than warm.

3. Add in the dry ingredients slowly, stirring as you go. Gradually it will come together to make a dough. Remove it from the heat and turn that dough out onto a prepared floured surface.

4. Knead the dough for at least 10 minutes, or until it is stretchable and silken.

5. Return the mixture to the bowl and cover it loosely with either a wet cloth or some clingfilm. Let it rise for approximately 1 hr to 1 hr 30 minutes. The dough will double in size.

6. Preheat the oven to 190C//374F//gas mark 5.

7 Remove the dough from the bowl and knock the air out of it by turning it over on itself a few times but do not knead it.

8 Separate your dough into 12 portions and roll flat. Mix the rest of the butter and sugar together and smear it on the dough.

9 Place rolls on a baking tray and cook for 25-30 minutes.

10 Mix the last of the cinnamon and the icing sugar with water and drizzle over cooled rolls.

English Tea Loaf

MAKES 1 FRUIT LOAF OR 4-5 SERVINGS
PREP TIME: 20 MINS | COOK TIME: 45 MINS | TOTAL TIME: 1 HR 5 MINS
NET CARBS PER 2 SLICES: 47G//1.65OZ | PROTEIN: 5G//0.17OZ |
FIBER: 2G//0.07OZ | FAT: 1G//0.35OZ | KCAL: 279

INGREDIENTS

- ○ 110g//3.8oz softened butter
- ○ 110g//3.8oz caster sugar
- ○ 225g//8oz self-raising flour
- ○ A pinch of salt
- ○ 225g//8oz mixed dried fruit*
- ○ 2 large eggs. beaten
- ○ 20ml//0.67floz whole milk

*Can be substituted for chocolate

INSTRUCTIONS

1   Preheat the oven to 180C//356F//gas mark 4. Line a loaf tin or baking tray in preparation.

2   Cream the butter and the sugar together in a large bowl until the mixture is smooth.

3   Rub in the flour and the salt until the mixture forms a breadcrumb consistency.

4   Add the fruit into the mixture and stir well.

5   Add in the eggs and mix.

6   Place into the loaf tin or onto the baking tray and brush the dough with the milk.

7   bake for about 45 minutes or until it has turned golden.

8   Place it on a wire rack to cool for 15-20 minutes before cutting.

Light and Airy Brioche Loaf

MAKES 8 PORTIONS OR ONE LOAF
PREP TIME: 45 MINS (PLUS 3.5 HOURS PROOFING) |
COOK TIME: 35 MINS | TOTAL TIME: 4 HRS 50 MINS

NET CARBS PER PORTION: 49G//1.72OZ | PROTEIN: 12G//0.42OZ |
FIBER: 2G//0.07OZ | FAT: 23G//0.81OZ | KCAL: 460

INGREDIENTS

- ○ 7g//0.25oz dried active yeast
- ○ 50g//1.76oz sugar
- ○ 450g//15.8oz strong white bread flour
- ○ A pinch of sea salt
- ○ 100ml//3.34floz whole milk
- ○ 5 room temperature eggs, one beaten to glaze
- ○ 200g//7.05oz unsalted butter, softened

INSTRUCTIONS

1 Place the yeast, sugar, and flour in a bowl and mix. Add the salt last and stir well.

2 Heat the milk gently in a saucepan over a low heat.

3 Make a well in the centre of the flour mixture and gradually pour the warmed milk into the hole.

4   Beat your 4 eggs in one bowl and your fifth egg separately. Gradually add the 4 eggs to the mixture, stirring all the while.

5   Gradually feed in the butter while mixing. This recipe is best mixed with a hand mixer or electronic mixing bowl from this point forward. Beating by hand is possible but will take much longer. It should take 10 minutes to feed in the butter and eggs.

6   Line a large bowl with a little butter and place the dough into it. Cover it with cling film loosely and leave it to proof somewhere warm for up to two hours.

7   Place your risen dough in the fridge to chill for 1 hour or more.

8   Preheat your oven to 180C//356F//gas mark 4.

9   Turn the dough onto a floured surface and divide into 8 equal dough balls.

10   Place the dough balls into a lined loaf tin and brush them with the remaining egg.

11   Bake for 30-35 minutes and leave to cool for 15 minutes before serving.

Baked Starters//Appetizers

Baked Camembert

SERVES 4 PEOPLE
PREP TIME: 5 MINUTES | COOK TIME: 20 MINS | TOTAL TIME: 25 MINUTES
NET CARBS: 0.28G//0.009OZ | PROTEIN: 12.18G//0.43OZ |
FIBER: 0G//0OZ | FAT: 14.92G//0.52OZ | KCAL: 184

INGREDIENTS

- ❍ 1 round camembert cheese (250g//8.8 oz) *
- ❍ 1 sprig rosemary or thyme
- ❍ (optional) 1 teaspoon chilli flakes
- ❍ (optional) 1 teaspoon white wine

* Can be substituted with brie

INSTRUCTIONS

1   Preheat the oven to 180 C//356F//gas mark 5.

2   Remove the cheese from its plastic packaging and return it to its wooden container.

3   Slice cheese into 4 quarters, scoring two lines into the surface until you can see the cheese underneath the skin.

4   Place sprig of rosemary or thyme (depending on taste) along the central line.

5   Sprinkle drops of wine and optional chilli flakes over the cheese.

6   Place in the centre of your preheated oven and bake for 20 minutes or until the centre of the cheese has become gooey.

7   Serve with crackers, bread, or garlic bread.

Italian Garlic and Rosemary Focaccia

SERVES 2 PEOPLE
PREP TIME: 1 HR 5 MINS | TOTAL TIME: 1 HR 25 MINS
NET CARBS PER SLICE: 20G//0.70OZ | PROTEIN: 5G//0.17OZ |
FIBER: 1G//0.03OZ | FAT: 4.5G//0.16OZ | KCAL: 142

INGREDIENTS

- ○ 1 sachet dried yeast
- ○ A pinch of sugar
- ○ 300ml//10.1floz lukewarm water
- ○ 400g//14.14oz strong white bread flour
- ○ A pinch of salt
- ○ 20ml//0.7floz olive oil
- ○ 100g//3.50z semolina flour
- ○ Two sprigs rosemary, finely chopped
- ○ Two garlic cloves, crushed or finely chopped
- ○ A pinch of flaked sea salt

INSTRUCTIONS

1 Place the yeast and sugar in the jug of lukewarm water, stir it, and cover it. Place it somewhere warm, but not hot. Leave it for ten minutes to ferment.

2 Preheat your oven to 220C//428F//gas mark 7.

3 Mix your flour and salt together in a large bowl.

4 Make a well in the centre of your flour mix and add the yeast and water mix a little at a time. It will come together into a dough.

5 Turn the dough onto a lightly floured surface and knead for 10 minutes.

6 Use 10ml of olive oil to line a fresh bowl and transfer your dough into it. Cover it loosely with clingfilm and leave it for 30 minutes.

7 The dough will have risen to double in size. Turn it out onto a floured surface again, this time using the semolina flour. Turn it over on itself to knock the air out of the mixture.

8 Roll the dough out onto until it is about the thickness of a pound coin// dollar coin.

9 Transfer your flat dough onto a baking tray that has been lined with parchment paper.

10 Brush the dough with the remainder of the olive oil, the garlic, and rosemary. Sprinkle with the salt.

11 Cook for 15-20 minutes or until golden brown. Serve immediately.

Goats Cheese and Caramelized Red Onion Tart

MAKES 6 TARTS
PREP TIME: 35 MINS | COOK TIME: 15 MINS | TOTAL TIME: 50 MINS
NET CARBS PER TART: 26G//0.70OZ | PROTEIN: 7.9G//0.17OZ |
FIBER: 1.1G//0.04OZ | FAT: 21.5G//0.16OZ | KCAL: 336

INGREDIENTS

- ◯ 500g//17.63oz short crust Pastry
- ◯ 1 tbsp butter
- ◯ 20ml//0.7floz olive oil
- ◯ 3 red onions, finely diced
- ◯ 1 tbsp reduced balsamic vinegar
- ◯ 1 tsp thyme
- ◯ A pinch of salt
- ◯ 200g//7oz goat's cheese

INSTRUCTIONS

1 Preheat oven to 200C//392F//gas mark 6 and line your tart cases with butter.

2 Roll out your pastry and insert it into your tart cases.

3 Place parchment paper over the pastry and fill with baking beans or dried lentils to blind bake. Bake in the oven for 10 minutes, until the pastry is starting to brown and holds its shape on its own.

4 Leave the pastry to cool without removing them from the tart cases.

5 Heat the oil in a saucepan over a medium heat.

6 Add the finely chopped onion and the vinegar. Sprinkle in the thyme, add the salt, and lastly break in the goat's cheese.

7 Reduce the heat to a low setting and simmer for five minutes.

8 Once the cheese is beginning to melt, remove from the heat and spoon the mixture evenly into your tart cases.

9 Return tarts to the oven and bake for a further 15 minutes, or until your tarts are golden brown and melting.

10 Serve immediately.

Pull Apart Cheesy Garlic Flatbread

SERVES 4 PEOPLE
PREP TIME: 55 MINS | COOK TIME: 25 MINS | TOTAL TIME: 1 HR 20 MINS
NET CARBS PER 53G//1.86OZ PIECE: 12G//0.42OZ | PROTEIN: 6G//0.21OZ |
FIBER: 0.6G//0.04OZ | FAT: 14G//0.49OZ | KCAL: 199

INGREDIENTS (DOUGH)

- ○ 7g//0.24oz pack of dried yeast
- ○ 200ml//6.76floz lukewarm water
- ○ A pinch of sugar
- ○ 1 egg
- ○ 45g//1.5oz softened unsalted butter
- ○ 300g//10.5oz strong white bread flour
- ○ 2 tsp garlic powder
- ○ A pinch of salt

INGREDIENTS (TOPPING)

- ○ 75g//2.64oz melted butter
- ○ 2 minced garlic cloves
- ○ 2 tsp chopped rosemary or thyme (optional)
- ○ 2 tsp chopped parsley (optional)
- ○ 100g//3.5oz cheddar/parmesan/cheese of your choice
- ○ A pinch of flaked rock salt

INSTRUCTIONS

1 Start by making your dough. Mix the yeast with the lukewarm water and the sugar in a jug. Cover the bowl with clingfilm and set it aside for 15 minutes or until a froth forms.

2 Beat the egg in a large bowl, then add the butter, flour, garlic, and salt to that same bowl and mix it well.

3 Add the frothy yeast and mix until it is smooth. If you do not have a dough-like consistency, add more water to make it less stiff or more flour to make it stiffer.

4 Turn your dough onto a floured surface and stretch and knead it for ten minutes.

5 Return the dough to the bowl and cover it with cling film. Leave it somewhere warm to rise for 30 minutes or so.

6 Preheat the oven to 180C//356F//gas mark 4. Line a baking tray with parchment paper.

7 Take the dough from the bowl and turn it over on itself a few times to knock the air out.

8 Separate the dough into small balls, no larger than a table tennis ball. Place these on a lined baking tray.

9 Score a line through the centre on each of the balls and set them aside.

10 To make your filling, combine the melted butter, garlic, and optional ingredients into one small bowl.

11 Brush the mixture over your dough balls until you have used it all. Sprinkle the cheese on top of the dough, and finally sprinkle with the rock salt.

12 Place in the centre of the oven and bake for 20-25 minutes or until the cheese is starting to crisp. Serve while still hot.

Baked Pies and Main Meals

Classic Chicken and Mushroom Pie

SERVES 4/5 PEOPLE
PREP TIME: 45 MINS | COOK TIME: 35 MINS | TOTAL TIME: 1 HR 20 MINS

NET CARBS PER ¼ PIE: 57G//2.1OZ | PROTEIN: 55G//1.94OZ |
FIBER: 1G//0.035OZ | FAT: 47G//1.65OZ | KCAL: 855

INGREDIENTS

- ○ 2 tbsp oil
- ○ 6 sliced chicken breasts
- ○ 1 diced onion
- ○ 250g//8.8oz sliced mushrooms
- ○ A pinch of salt/pepper
- ○ 1 tbsp thyme
- ○ 2 tbsp flour
- ○ 350ml//11.8floz chicken stock
- ○ 180ml//6floz milk
- ○ 500g//17.63oz fresh puff pastry
- ○ 1 beaten egg

INSTRUCTIONS

1 Heat the oil in a saucepan over a medium heat and add your sliced chicken. Cook until seared white.

2 Add the onion, mushrooms, salt and pepper, and thyme to the pan. Cook for a further five minutes stirring often. Add the flour and cook for another few minutes.

3 Add the chicken stock and remove the saucepan from the heat. While it is cooling, stir in the milk and return it to a low heat. Cover and simmer the entire mixture for 30 minutes.

4 Preheat the oven to 220C//428F//gas mark 7.

5 Roll out your pastry while the pan is cooking and line your pie tin with a brush of butter and parchment paper. Make sure your pastry is 1/5 an inch thick or more. You may use the extra pastry to decorate the pie lid.

6 Gently spoon the cooked mixture from the pan to the pie case. Place the lid on and glaze with the egg.

7 Put your pie in the oven and bake for thirty minutes or until golden brown and risen.

Vegetarian Shepherd's Pie

SERVES 4/5 PEOPLE
PREP TIME: 10 MINS | COOK TIME: 1 HR | TOTAL TIME: 1 HR 10 MINS
NET CARBS PER ¼ PIE: 66G//2.1OZ | PROTEIN: 16G//1.94OZ |
FIBER: 16G//0.035OZ | FAT: 15G//1.65OZ | KCAL: 530

INGREDIENTS

- ○ 1 tbsp olive oil
- ○ 1 large onion, peeled and chopped
- ○ 2 large carrots, peeled and chopped
- ○ 1 can chopped tomatoes (440g//15.5oz)
- ○ 1 can lentils (400g//14.1oz)
- ○ 1 vegetable stock cube
- ○ 150ml//5.1floz boiling water
- ○ 200ml//6.76floz red wine
- ○ 900g//31.7oz potatoes, peeled and chopped
- ○ 30g//1.05oz butter
- ○ A pinch of salt and pepper
- ○ 100g//3.5oz cheese of your choice
- ○ 2 tbsp chopped rosemary or thyme (optional)
- ○ 500g//17.6oz short crust pastry, ready to roll

INSTRUCTIONS

1   Put the oil in a frying pan and heat on a low heat. When it is hot enough to sizzle, add the onion. Gently heat the onions until they are caramelised/browned. Add the chopped carrots, the tomatoes, and the lentils.

2   In a separate jug, mix the stock cubes into the boiling water and add to the frying pan. Pour in the red wine and add in the optional rosemary or thyme. Allow ingredients to simmer.

3   Place the potatoes in a saucepan with some water and bring them to the boil for 15 minutes. Remove from the heat and drain, then mash in the butter. Add salt and pepper to taste.

4   Preheat your oven to 190C//374F//gas mark 5 and roll out your pastry to fit your pie tin. The pastry should be about ¼ inch thick.

5   Spoon your ingredients into the pie case, cover with mash, and bake for 20 minutes.

Old English Steak and Ale pie

SERVES 4/5 PEOPLE
PREP TIME: 25 MINS | COOK TIME: 1 HR 20 MINS | TOTAL TIME: 1 HR 45 MINS

NET CARBS PER ¼ PIE: 46G//1.6OZ | PROTEIN:58G//2.04OZ |
FIBER: 6G//0.21OZ | FAT: 54G//1.90OZ | KCAL: 923

INGREDIENTS

- ❍ 1 tbsp olive oil
- ❍ 900g//31.74oz raw steak, diced
- ❍ 2 large onions, diced
- ❍ 2 large carrots, chopped
- ❍ 150g//5.29oz sliced mushrooms
- ❍ 2 tsp thyme
- ❍ 400ml//13.5floz beef stock
- ❍ 400ml//13.5floz strong black ale
- ❍ 350g//12.3oz fresh puff pastry
- ❍ 25g//0.8ozg butter
- ❍ Salt and pepper to taste
- ❍ 1 beaten egg

INSTRUCTIONS

1 Heat the oil in a saucepan over a medium heat and place in the steak. Cook until it is seared on all sides.

2 Add in each of the vegetables and the thyme.

3 Add in the stock and ale and allow to simmer for 1 hour, covered and on a low heat.

4 While the mix is cooking, roll out your pastry. Line your pie tin with butter and parchment paper and place your pastry in the dish. Keep some for the lid.

5 Preheat your oven to 220C//428F//gas mark 7.

6 Season your pie mixture with salt and pepper before you remove it from the heat.

7 Gently spoon the mixture into your pie case and cover it with a pastry lid. Seal the pie closed with the egg. Brush the pie with the mix to glaze.

8 Cool for 30 minutes or until golden brown.

Country Cottage pie

SERVES 4/5 PEOPLE
PREP TIME: 25 MINS | COOK TIME: 30 MINS | TOTAL TIME: 55 MINS
NET CARBS PER ¼ PIE: 20G//0.7OZ | PROTEIN:16G//0.56OZ |
FIBER: 5G//0.17OZ | FAT: 35G//1.2OZ | KCAL: 658

INGREDIENTS

- ❍ 900g//31.74oz potatoes, peeled and diced
- ❍ 1 tbsp olive oil
- ❍ 1 large onion, finely diced
- ❍ 2 carrots, thinly sliced
- ❍ 1 small tin garden peas (150g//5.29oz)
- ❍ 1 celery stalk, diced
- ❍ 500g//17.6oz lean beef mince
- ❍ 2 bay leaves
- ❍ 1 tin chopped tomato (400g//14.10oz)
- ❍ 20g//0.70oz tomato puree
- ❍ 150ml//5.07floz beef stock
- ❍ A pinch of salt
- ❍ 30g//1.05oz butter

INSTRUCTIONS

1   Place your potatoes in a pan of salted water and bring them to the boil.

2   Preheat oven to 180C//356F//gas mark 4.

3   Heat the oil in a frying pan over a medium heat. When the oil is hot, add the onion, carrots, peas, celery, and beef. Allow the beef to brown.

4   Add in the bay leaves, tomatoes, tomato puree, and the beef stock. Allow to simmer for 15 minutes.

5   Remove your potatoes from the heat, drain them, add in salt and butter and mash.

6   Remove bay leaves from the meat mixture and discard. Then place the mixture into an oven proof dish.

7   Spoon mash on top and place in the oven. Cook for 20 minutes or until golden brown.

Succulent Shepherd's Pie

SERVES 4/5
PREP TIME: 20 MINS | COOK TIME: 45 MINS | TOTAL TIME: 1 HR 5 MINS
NET CARBS PER ¼ PIE: 52G//1.83OZ | PROTEIN:34G//1.19OZ |
FIBER: 6.7G//0.23OZ | FAT: 40G//1.41OZ | KCAL: 693

INGREDIENTS

- ◯ 900g//31.74oz potatoes
- ◯ 2 tbsp olive oil
- ◯ 1 large, diced onion
- ◯ 550g//19.4oz raw minced lamb
- ◯ 250g// 8.8oz diced vegetables of your choice (carrots, peas, mange tout, green beans)
- ◯ 100ml//3.38floz beef stock
- ◯ 25g//0.88oz gravy browning
- ◯ 2 tbsp Worcestershire sauce
- ◯ Salt and pepper to taste
- ◯ 60g//2.11oz salted butter
- ◯ (Optional) 25g//0.88oz cheese

INSTRUCTIONS

1   Peel and chop your potatoes, place them in a pan with salted water. Bring them to the boil for 15-20 minutes.

2   Preheat your oven to 200C//392F//gas mark 6.

3   Place the oil into a frying pan and gently heat on a medium setting. Add in the onions.

4   Add the lamb to the pan and allow it to brown.

5   Add the diced vegetables to the pan and heat for a few minutes.

6   Mix your beef stock with your gravy browning and the Worcester sauce in a separate jug. Add it slowly to the mixture in the frying pan. Simmer for five minutes then turn the frying pan to a low heat.

7   Remove the potatoes from the heat and drain them. Put them back into the pot. Add salt and pepper to taste, and your butter. Mash the potato until it is smooth.

8 Spoon the frying pan contents into an oven proof dish and add the mashed potato as a pie lid. Optionally, you can add a sprinkle of cheese here for a crisper crust.

9 Place in the oven and cook for 30 minutes or until the mash has turned golden.

Baked Salmon

MAKES 1 PORTION
PREP TIME: 15 MINS | COOK TIME: 15 MINS | TOTAL TIME: 30 MINS
NET CARBS PER ¼ PIE: 52G//1.83OZ | PROTEIN:34G//1.19OZ |
FIBER: 6.7G//0.23OZ | FAT: 40G//1.41OZ | KCAL: 693

INGREDIENTS

- ○ 1 piece of salmon
- ○ A knob of butter
- ○ 1 half lemon
- ○ A pinch of salt
- ○ A sprinkle of dill
- ○ Optional substitutes for dill/ lemon include garlic, parsley, thyme, fennel seeds, rosemary, pesto, or other preferred herb/spice.
- ○ Optional substitutes for salmon include haddock, cod, hake, bass, or other fish of choice.

INSTRUCTIONS

1   Preheat the oven to 200C//392F//gas mark 6.

2   Select the salmon piece and prepare it by removing any bones or skin.

3   Place your piece of fish inside a square of cooking foil.

4   Place the knob of butter and the salt, lemon, and dill inside the foil.

5   Close the fish inside the foil so there are no gaps.

6   Place foiled fish onto a wire rack to cook, directly inside the oven.

7   Leave fish to bake for 10 minutes and serve.

Baked Chicken Parmigiana

MAKES 4 PORTIONS
PREP TIME: 15 MINS | COOK TIME: 15 MINS | TOTAL TIME: 30 MINS

NET CARBS PER PORTION: 22G//0.77OZ | PROTEIN:33G//1.16OZ |
FIBER: 1G//0.03OZ | FAT: 13G//0.45OZ | KCAL: 327

INGREDIENTS

- ◯ 100g//3.52oz flour
- ◯ 2 large beaten eggs
- ◯ 75g//2.64oz panko breadcrumbs
- ◯ 3 large chicken breasts
- ◯ 1 tbsp olive oil
- ◯ 2 diced garlic cloves
- ◯ 700ml//23.66floz passata sauce
- ◯ 1 tbsp sugar
- ◯ 1 tsp Italian herb seasoning/mixed herbs
- ◯ 70g//2.46oz grated Italian hard cheese/parmesan
- ◯ 1 ball mozzarella

INSTRUCTIONS

1 Add flour to one bowl, breadcrumbs to a second bowl, and place beaten eggs in a third.

2 Cut your chicken breasts in half along the width in a butterfly cut. Place between two sheets of clingfilm and bash with a meat hammer or a rolling pin. Bash the breast halves until they are flat.

3 Dip the chicken in flour, then in egg, then in breadcrumbs, leave to dry then repeat with a second coat. You do not need the flour the second time.

4 Heat the oil in a frying pan then add in the garlic and the passata sauce. Add in the sugar, mixed herbs, and season. Simmer for ten minutes.

5 While that is cooking, place the chicken under the grill to crisp for five minutes on each side.

6 Preheat your oven to 200C//392F//gas mark 6.

7 Put the chicken into an oven proof dish and spoon in the sauce. Make sure there is sauce underneath the chicken. Sprinkle on hard cheese and thinly slice the mozzarella ball and place the circles on top.

8 Bake for 20-25 minutes or until it is gooey and delicious. Serve immediately.

Baked Biscuits//Cookies

Dropped Scones/Biscuits

MAKES 8 SCONES
PREP TIME: 15 MINS | COOK TIME: 15 MINS | TOTAL TIME: 30 MINS

NET CARBS PER PORTION: 22G//0.77OZ | PROTEIN:33G//1.16OZ |
FIBER: 1G//0.03OZ | FAT: 13G//0.45OZ | KCAL: 327

INGREDIENTS

- ○ 55g//2oz butter
- ○ 30g//1.2oz sugar
- ○ 225g//8oz self-raising flour
- ○ A pinch of salt
- ○ 150ml//5floz whole milk

INSTRUCTIONS

1   Preheat your oven to 220C//428F//gas mark 7.

2   Cream the butter and sugar together in a large bowl.

3   Rub the flour into the butter and sugar mix and add the pinch of salt.

4   Add the milk a little at a time until the dough starts to come together.

5   Turn the dough onto a floured surface and roll to 2-inch thickness.

6   Cut out circles for your scones. You can use a cutter or a cup.

7   Place on a lined baking tray and brush with milk.

8   Place in the oven for 15-20 mins or until golden brown.

Traditional Scottish Shortbread Recipe

MAKES 20 INDIVIDUAL SHORTBREAD TRIANGLES
PREP TIME: 15 MINS | COOK TIME: 20 MINS | TOTAL TIME: 35 MINS

NET CARBS PER 2 BISCUITS: 16G//0.56OZ | PROTEIN: 2G//0.07OZ |
FIBER: 0.6G//0.021OZ | FAT: 4G//0.14OZ | KCAL: 156

INGREDIENTS

- ○ 100g butter, softened
- ○ 50g caster sugar plus dusting
- ○ 150g plain flour

INSTRUCTIONS

1   Preheat your oven to 170C//338F//gas mark 3 and line a baking tray.

2   Cream the butter and sugar together in a large mixing bowl.

3   Rub in the flour then press together into a dough.

4   Turn out the dough on a lightly floured surface.

5   Roll out shortbread dough to 1 inch thick.

6   Use a plate to mark circular biscuits and score with 4 lines through the centre.

7   Bake for 20 minutes or until golden.

8   Separate the biscuits when they are warm.

Chocolate Chip Cookies

MAKES 10 COOKIES
PREP TIME: 20 MINS | COOK TIME: 15 MINS | TOTAL TIME: 35 MINS
NET CARBS PER COOKIE: 16G//0.56OZ | PROTEIN: 3G//0.105OZ |
FIBER: 2G//0.070OZ | FAT: 16G//0.56OZ | KCAL: 308

INGREDIENTS

- ○ 120g//4.23oz softened butter
- ○ 75g//2.64oz light brown sugar
- ○ 75g//2.64oz muscovado sugar
- ○ 1 large egg
- ○ 2 drops vanilla extract
- ○ 180g//6.34oz plain flour
- ○ 1 tsp bicarbonate of soda
- ○ A pinch of salt
- ○ 150g//5.3oz chocolate chips/chunks*

* You may use any kind of chocolate for this. Chocolate could be replaced with fudge.

INSTRUCTIONS

1   Preheat oven to 180C//356F//gas mark 4.

2   Cream the butter and sugars together until the mixture is smooth.

3   Beat in the egg and vanilla extract using a fork or metal spoon.

4   Sieve in the flour and fold it into the mixture, add the bicarbonate of soda.

5   Add the pinch of salt and the chocolate and mix well.

6   Prepare 4 baking sheets by lining them with parchment paper.

7   Scoop equal amounts of mixture onto the sheets. Space them out.

8   Place the cookie dough into the oven and bake for 15 minutes.

9   The cookies will spread out and turn golden brown.

Viennese Whirls

MAKES 10 BISCUITS
PREP TIME: 45 MINS | COOK TIME: 15 MINS | TOTAL TIME: 1 HR
NET CARBS PER 2 BISCUITS: 42G//1.48 OZ | PROTEIN: 2G//0.0705OZ |
FIBER: 1G//0.035OZ | FAT: 25G//0.88OZ | KCAL: 405

INGREDIENTS (BISCUITS)

- ◯ 200g//7.05oz salted butter, softened
- ◯ 50g//1.7oz icing sugar
- ◯ 2 drops vanilla extract
- ◯ 200g//7.05oz plain flour
- ◯ 1 tbsp corn flour
- ◯ 1 tsp baking powder

INGREDIENTS (FILLING)

- ◯ 100g//3.52oz softened unsalted butter
- ◯ 150g//5.29oz icing sugar
- ◯ 30g//1.05oz jam of your choice (usually strawberry)

INSTRUCTIONS

1 Preheat your oven to 180C//356F//gas mark 4 and line two baking trays with parchment.

2 Mix the butter, vanilla extract, and icing sugar together in a large bowl using an electric whisk.

3 Sieve the flour, corn flour, and baking powder. Fold these dry ingredients into the mixture.

4 Put dough into a piping bag and pipe swirls onto the lined trays.

5 Bake for 15 minutes or until golden.

6 Remove from the oven and cool on a wire cooling rack for 20 minutes or more.

7 While cooling, add butter and icing sugar to a bowl and cream them together.

8 Each biscuit is then coated with jam, given a layer of cream, and stuck to another.

Ginger Snap Biscuits

MAKES 10 BISCUITS
PREP TIME: 15 MINS | COOK TIME: 35 MINS | TOTAL TIME: 50 MINS
NET CARBS PER BISCUIT: 5G//0.17 OZ | PROTEIN: 1G//0.035OZ |
FIBER: 1G//0.035OZ | FAT:5G//0.17OZ | KCAL: 120

INGREDIENTS

- ○ 150g//5.29oz softened butter
- ○ 75g//2.64oz soft brown sugar
- ○ 75g//2.64oz muscovado sugar
- ○ 2 tbsp golden syrup
- ○ 150g//5.29oz plain flour
- ○ 1 tbsp baking powder
- ○ 2 tbsp ground ginger
- ○ 1tbsp ground cinnamon

INSTRUCTIONS

1   Preheat the oven to 170C//338F//gas mark 3.

2   Line two baking trays with parchment paper.

3   Cream together the butter and the sugars in a large mixing bowl.

4   Add the syrup and beat until you have a smooth, silken consistency.

5   Gradually sieve in the flour, baking powder, and spices.

6   Fold the dry ingredients into the mixture slowly.

7   The mix should come to a dough stiff enough to roll into balls.

8   Portion out the mixture, roll into balls, then squash onto the lined trays.

9   Bake in the oven for 20 minutes or until golden brown.

10   Leave an extra 5-10 minutes for a crisper biscuit.

11   Allow to cool for 15-20 minutes and serve.

Country Oat Biscuits

MAKES 12 BISCUITS
PREP TIME: 15 MINS | COOK TIME: 15 MINS | TOTAL TIME: 30 MINS

NET CARBS PER BISCUIT: 17G//0.59 OZ | PROTEIN: 2G//0.070OZ |
FIBER: 1G//0.035OZ | FAT:7G//0.246OZ | KCAL: 140

INGREDIENTS

- ○ 75g//2.64oz wholemeal flour
- ○ 80g//2.82oz oats
- ○ 50g//1.76oz granulated sugar
- ○ 1 tsp baking powder
- ○ 75g//2.64oz butter
- ○ 1 tbsp golden syrup
- ○ 2 tbsp milk

INSTRUCTIONS

1. Heat up your oven to 180C//356F//gas mark 4.

2. Line two baking trays with parchment paper.

3. Sieve your flour into a large bowl and add in the oats and sugar.

4. Mix the baking powder in and stir well.

5. Heat a saucepan on a low heat and melt the butter, syrup, and milk.

6. Once the mixture is completely melted, add it to the dry ingredients.

7. Stir everything until it is coated.

8. Portion with a tablespoon and space out cookies on your baking trays.

9. Place into the oven and bake for 10-15 minutes, or until golden brown.

Empire Biscuits

MAKES 12 BISCUITS
PREP TIME: 1 HR | COOK TIME: 15 MINS | TOTAL TIME: 1 HR 15 MINS
NET CARBS PER BISCUIT: 59G//2.08OZ | PROTEIN: 2G//0.70OZ |
FAT: 7G//0.24OZ | FIBER: 1G//0.035OZ | KCAL: 305

INGREDIENTS

- ○ 100g//3.5oz salted butter, softened
- ○ 300g//10.58oz icing sugar
- ○ 2 drops vanilla extract
- ○ 180g//6.34oz plain flour
- ○ 2 large eggs, yolks only
- ○ 5 tbsp strawberry jam
- ○ 50g//1.7oz tub of glacé cherries

INSTRUCTIONS

1 Cream the butter and 100g//3.5oz of the icing sugar together in a large bowl then stir in the vanilla extract.

2 Rub in the flour. Aim for a breadcrumb texture.

3 Beat the egg yolks and add them into the mixture. The mix should come together as a dough. If it is too dry, add a splash of milk. If it is too wet, add a little extra flour.

4 Tip the dough onto a lightly floured surface and knead for 2 minutes. Place it back into the bowl and cover with clingfilm. Put the bowl in the fridge to chill for half an hour, or until it is properly cold.

5 Remove the dough from the chill and preheat your oven to 180C//356F//gas mark 4.

6 Roll out the dough until it is the thickness of a pound/dollar coin.

7 Cut as many circular biscuits from the dough as you can, you should end up with 24 rounds.

8 Bake for 10-15 minutes or until golden brown.

9 Remove from the oven and allow to cool while you mix the remainder of your icing sugar with water.

10 To assemble your biscuits, coat one side in jam and sandwich together with a second biscuit. Icing sugar is then drizzled on top and a cherry is added. Remember not to add your icing sugar until the biscuits are cooled.

Baked Parmesan Tuiles

MAKES 10 TUILES
PREP TIME: 10 MINS | COOK TIME: 10 MINS | TOTAL TIME: 20 MINS
NET CARBS PER TUILE: 6G//0.21OZ | PROTEIN: 0G//0.00OZ |
FAT: 1G//0.035OZ | FIBER: 1G//0.035OZ | KCAL: 43

INGREDIENTS

- ○ 200g//7oz parmesan cheese or hard cheese equivalent
- ○ (Optional) 1 sprig rosemary, chopped

INSTRUCTIONS

1   Preheat your oven to 200C//392F//gas mark 6.

2   Grate the parmesan cheese on the finest part of your grater. If you have an electronic blender, reduce the parmesan to small particles by pulsing the cheese. If it gets too hot, you will cook it.

3   Line a baking tray with parchment paper.

4   Arrange the grated parmesan on the parchment paper in ten neat circles. You can shape the tuiles as you wish, but circles will impress your friends. Using a cheesecake mould can help. Sprinkle with chopped rosemary when prepared.

5   Place the tuiles into the oven and set a timer for ten minutes.

6   Remove from the oven and allow to cool. You should be able to pop the tuiles free of the parchment paper. They will resemble crisps.

Saltwater Crackers

MAKES 15 BISCUITS
PREP TIME: 25 MINS | COOK TIME: 15 MINS | TOTAL TIME: 40 MINS
NET CARBS PER BISCUIT: 9G//0.31OZ | PROTEIN: 1G//0.035OZ |
FAT: 2G//0.070OZ | FIBER: 0G//0OZ | KCAL: 60

INGREDIENTS

- ○ 200g//7oz plain flour
- ○ 1 teaspoon baking powder
- ○ 50g//1.76oz salted butter, softened
- ○ 20ml//0.67floz cold water
- ○ 30g//1oz Himalayan rock salt/flaked sea salt

INSTRUCTIONS

1 Preheat oven to 180C//356F//gas mark 4.

2 Mix the flour and baking powder together in a large bowl.

3 Rub in the butter, aiming for a breadcrumb consistency. If using a food processor, pulse the power on and off to avoid cooking the butter.

4 Use a dribble of water to bring the mixture together into a dough. You may not need all the water and you may need to add a little extra flour if it is too wet.

5 Turn the dough out onto a lightly floured surface.

6 Roll the dough until it is as thin as you can get it. Brush it with water and then sprinkle it with the salt. Make sure you press the salt into the dough, so it is not lost in the cooking process.

7 Bake in the oven for 15 minutes, remove and place on a wire rack to cool.

8 Once cooled, store in an airtight container for up to a fortnight.

Cakes and Desserts

Victoria Sandwich Cake

MAKES 6 PORTIONS OR ONE ROUND LOAF
PREP TIME: 30 MINS | COOK TIME: 25 MINS | TOTAL TIME: 55 MINS
NET CARBS PER PORTION: 50G//1.76OZ | PROTEIN: 5G//0.17OZ |
FAT: 31G//1.090OZ | FIBER: 0.5G//0.017OZ | KCAL: 500

INGREDIENTS

- ○ 4 large eggs
- ○ 225g//8oz softened butter
- ○ 225g//8oz caster sugar
- ○ 225g//8oz self-raising flour
- ○ 1 tsp baking powder
- ○ 100g//3.5oz strawberry or raspberry jam
- ○ Clotted or whipped cream (optional)
- ○ Icing sugar for dusting

INSTRUCTIONS

1 Preheat the oven to 180C//356F//gas mark 4 and line 2 cake tins with parchment paper. You can use one cake tin and cut the sponge in half, but two cake tins are better.

2 Using a hand mixer or a whisk, beat the eggs, butter, and sugar together in a bowl.

3 Gradually fold in the sieved flour and baking powder.

4 Divide the mix between the two lined cake tins and pop them in the oven for approximately 25 minutes.

5 Remove from the oven and place on a wire rack to cool. If you are using one cake tin and cutting the sponge in half, allow it to fully cool before you do so. Allowing cakes to cool inside the tins will make them less likely to break when you remove them.

6 Remove the cakes from their tins and slather the flat side of each with the jam. Sandwich the two pieces together.

7 You can either dust the cake with icing sugar to finish it or make up 50g//1.7oz icing sugar with a little water to drizzle it on top.

Carrot & Walnut Cake

MAKES 1 CAKE OR 8 PORTIONS
PREP TIME: 30 MINS | COOK TIME 35 MINS | TOTAL TIME: 1 HR 5 MINS
NET CARBS PER PORTION: 53G//1.8OZ | PROTEIN: 3.8G//0.13OZ |
FAT: 20.8G//0.70OZ | FIBER: 1.1G//0.038OZ | KCAL: 408

INGREDIENTS

- ○ 300g//10.5oz self-raising flour
- ○ 225g//8oz light brown sugar
- ○ 1 tbsp baking powder
- ○ 1 tsp ground ginger
- ○ 1 tsp mixed spice
- ○ 75g//2.6oz smashed walnuts
- ○ 200g//7oz peeled and grated carrot
- ○ 5 medium eggs, beaten
- ○ 2 drops vanilla essence
- ○ 50g//1.7oz softened butter
- ○ 250g//8.8oz cream cheese (whole fat)
- ○ 25g//0.88oz icing sugar

INSTRUCTIONS

1 Preheat the oven to 180C//356F//gas mark 4. Line two 8-inch cake tins with parchment paper and grease with a little butter to hold it in place.

2 Mix all the dry ingredients in a bowl, then add the walnuts, carrots, and eggs. The batter should be wet rather than stiff.

3 Divide the mixture evenly between the two cake tins and cook for 30-35 minutes, or until it is rounded and golden brown.

4 Remove from the oven and leave to cool on a wire rack until completely cold.

5 While it is cooling, mix the softened butter, cream cheese, vanilla essence and icing sugar in a bowl. This is your filling.

6 When the cake is cooled, smear filling on the two flat sides and sandwich together. Smear filling on top and around the edges of your cake, too.

Chocolate Cake

MAKES 12 PORTIONS
PREP TIME: 1 HR 30 MINS | COOK TIME 45 MINS | TOTAL TIME: 2 HRS 15 MINS
NET CARBS PER PORTION: 56G//1.97OZ | PROTEIN: 6.5G//0.22OZ |
FAT: 25G//0.88OZ | FIBER: 2.5G//0.088OZ | KCAL: 408

INGREDIENTS

- ○ 225g//8oz plain flour
- ○ 85g//3oz cocoa powder
- ○ 350g//12.34oz caster sugar
- ○ 2 tsp baking powder
- ○ 2 tsp bicarbonate of soda
- ○ 2 large eggs, beaten
- ○ 250ml//9floz whole milk
- ○ 125ml//4.22floz sunflower oil

INGREDIENTS (TOPPING)

- ○ 200g//7oz cooking chocolate
- ○ 200ml//7floz double cream
- ○ 250ml//9floz boiling water

INSTRUCTIONS

1   Preheat your oven to 180C//356F//gas mark 4 and line 2 8-inch cake tins.

2   Mix the dry ingredients in a large mixing bowl.

3   Stir in the beaten eggs, milk, and oil.

4   Divide the batter between the cake tins and bake for 35 mins.

5   Remove from oven and allow the cakes to cool on a wire rack.

6   Melt the chocolate and the cream together over the hot water on a low heat.

7   Let the cream and chocolate set for about an hour in the fridge.

8   Smear over the cake to sandwich together. Use this as a topping.

Marvellous Madeira Cake

MAKES 1 LOAF CAKE OR 8 SLICES
PREP TIME: 20 MINS | COOK TIME: 1 HR | TOTAL TIME: 1 HR 20 MINS
NET CARBS PER PORTION: 40G//1.41OZ | PROTEIN: 6G//0.21OZ |
FAT: 24G//0.084OZ | FIBER: 1.4G//0.49OZ | KCAL: 397

INGREDIENTS

- ◯ 3 large eggs
- ◯ 100g//3.5oz caster sugar
- ◯ 75g//2.6oz soft brown sugar
- ◯ 3 drops vanilla essence
- ◯ The zest and juice of half a lemon
- ◯ 200g//7oz self-raising flour
- ◯ 50g//1.7oz ground almonds

INSTRUCTIONS

1   Use a 900g//31oz loaf tin, grease and line it with parchment paper. Preheat your oven to 170C//338F//gas mark 3.

2   Beat the sugars and the eggs in with whisk. A hand mixer would be best for this.

3   Add the vanilla and lemon zest and juice, then start folding in the dry ingredients. Add the almonds last.

4   Place the mixture into a lined cake tin and bake in the oven for an hour.

5   Remove from the oven when golden and spongey, then allow to cool for 20 minutes before slicing.

Ruby Red Velvet Cake

MAKES 8 PORTIONS OR ONE ROUND CAKE
PREP TIME: 1 HR 30 MINS | COOK TIME: 30 MINS | TOTAL TIME: 2 HOURS
NET CARBS PER PORTION: 36G//1.26OZ | PROTEIN:4G//0.14OZ |
FAT: 23G//0.81OZ | FIBER: 0.3G//0.010OZ | KCAL: 368

INGREDIENTS

- 300g//10.5oz self-raising flour
- 22g//0.77oz cocoa powder
- A teaspoon of baking powder
- A pinch of salt
- 115g//4oz unsalted butter, softened
- 350g//12.34oz caster sugar
- 2 large room temperature eggs
- 120ml//4floz vegetable oil
- 2 tsp red food colouring
- 1 tsp white wine vinegar
- 320ml//10.8floz whole milk

INGREDIENTS (TOPPING)

- 340g//12oz cream cheese (whole fat)
- 175g//6.17oz softened butter
- 360g//12.7oz icing sugar
- 2 tsp vanilla essence

INSTRUCTIONS

1. Preheat the oven to 180C//356F//gas mark 4. Line two 9-inch cake tins with parchment paper.

2. Whisk the flour, cocoa powder, baking powder and salt in a bowl, then sieve them together.

3. In a second bowl, cream 115g//4oz of the butter together with the caster sugar and beat in the eggs.

4. beat in the oil, the food colouring, the vinegar, and the milk.

5. Fold in the dry ingredients we set aside earlier.

6. Distribute the mixture between the tins evenly.

7. Place inside the oven and bake for 30 minutes.

8. Remove from the oven and leave to cool.

9. Mix the creamed cheese, leftover butter, icing sugar and vanilla for the frosting.

Coffee Cake

MAKES 1 ROUND CAKE OR 8 PORTIONS
PREP TIME: 20 MINS | COOK TIME 30 MINS | TOTAL TIME: 50 MINS
NET CARBS PER PORTION: 66G//2.32OZ | PROTEIN: 5G//0.17OZ |
FAT:30G//1.05OZ | FIBER: 1G//0.35OZ | KCAL: 559

INGREDIENTS

- ○ 170g//6oz unsalted butter, softened
- ○ 170g//6oz caster sugar
- ○ 170g//6oz self-raising flour
- ○ 3 large eggs, beaten.
- ○ 1 tbsp instant coffee, dissolved in 1 tbsp boiling water

INGREDIENTS (ICING)

- ○ 22g//0.77oz icing sugar
- ○ 100g//3.5oz unsalted butter, softened
- ○ 2 tbsp instant coffee, dissolved in 2 tbsp boiling water

INSTRUCTIONS

1. Preheat your oven to 180C//356F//gas mark 4. Line two 8-inch sandwich tins.

2. Whisk the butter and sugar until creamy and beat in the eggs, using a little flour with each egg. Add the rest of the flour and fold it in.

3. Fold in the coffee.

4. Divide the mixture between the two cake tins and place in the oven to bake for 30 minutes.

5. Remove from the oven and allow to cool on a wire rack.

6. While it is cooling, blend the icing sugar with the unsalted butter and the second lot of coffee, and mix together.

7. Smear on the flat sides of the two cakes and press the sponges together. You may use jam if you prefer.

8. Coat the cake in as much of the topping as you can and enjoy.

Baked New York Cheesecake

MAKES 16 PORTIONS
**PREP TIME: 30 MINS | COOK TIME: 2 HR 25 MINS (PLUS OVERNIGHT
CHILLING TIME) | TOTAL TIME: 2 HRS 55 MINS**
NET CARBS PER PORTION: 33G//1.16OZ | PROTEIN: 6G//0.21OZ |
FAT:18G//0.63OZ | FIBER: 1G//0.35OZ | KCAL: 320

INGREDIENTS (BASE)

- ◯ 200g//7oz plain flour
- ◯ 125g//4.5oz unsalted softened butter
- ◯ 1 large beaten egg
- ◯ 25g//0.88oz caster sugar

INGREDIENTS (CAKE)

- ◯ 1200g//42oz creamed cheese, whole fat and softened
- ◯ 350g//12oz caster sugar
- ◯ 5 eggs plus 2 egg yolks, instructions on how to separate are here
- ◯ 15g//0.17oz plain flour
- ◯ 60ml//2floz double cream

INSTRUCTIONS

1 Preheat your oven to 200C//392F//gas mark 6 and grease and line a 25 cm diameter cake tin.

2 Combine all the ingredients for the base and mix well. Put the base mix into the tin and press it down to the bottom so that it is flat. Prick it with a knife a few times and place it in the oven to bake for about 15 minutes.

3 Remove it from the oven and let it cool. Turn your oven up to 240C//464F//gas mark 9.

4 Beat all the cheesecake ingredients together except for the cream. Add the cream all in one go and stop stirring as soon as it is mixed in.

5 When the base is cool, pour the mixture over the base and shake the pan so that it falls to the bottom.

6 Put into the oven and bake for 10 mins at 240C//464F//gas mark 9, then bring the temperature right down to 110C//230F//gas mark ¼.

7 Bake the cheesecake at this low temperature for about an hour.

8 Turn off the oven and leave the cake in there until it is completely cool.

9 Remove the baked New York cheesecake and chill overnight before eating.

Pineapple Upside Down Cake

MAKES 6 PORTIONS OR ONE ROUND CAKE
PREP TIME: 15 MINS | COOK TIME: 40 MINS | TOTAL TIME: 55 MINS
NET CARBS PER PORTION: 49G//1.7OZ | PROTEIN: 5G//0.17OZ |
FAT:23G//0.81OZ | FIBER: 1G//0.35OZ | KCAL: 407

INGREDIENTS (TOPPING)

- ◯ 50g//1.7 oz softened unsalted butter
- ◯ 50g//1.7oz soft brown sugar
- ◯ 1 tin pineapple rings
- ◯ 1 tub glacé cherries

INGREDIENTS

- ◯ 100g//3.5oz softened unsalted butter
- ◯ 100g//3.5oz caster sugar
- ◯ 1 tsp vanilla essence
- ◯ 2 large eggs
- ◯ 100g//3.5oz self-raising flour
- ◯ 1 tsp baking powder

INSTRUCTIONS

1. Preheat your oven to 180C//356F//gas mark 4 and grease and line a 20cm cake tin.

2. Mix the topping's butter and sugar together and use it to coat the inside of the cake tin. Cover the sticky mixture with the pineapple rings and place a cherry in the centre of each ring. It should take about 7 rings to cover your cake.

3. Cream the butter and sugar together in a bowl with the vanilla essence.

4. Beat in the 2 large eggs.

5. Fold in the sieved flour and baking powder.

6. Pour this batter into the cake tin, on top of the pineapple rings and cherries.

7. Place in the centre of your oven and bake for 35 mins or until golden brown.

8. Leave the cake to cool for about 15 minutes before turning it out onto a cooling rack. You should see the pineapple and cherries on the top.

Disclaimer

This book contains opinions and ideas of the author and is meant to teach the reader informative and helpful knowledge while due care should be taken by the user in the application of the information provided. The instructions and strategies are possibly not right for every reader and there is no guarantee that they work for everyone. Using this book and implementing the information/recipes therein contained is explicitly your own responsibility and risk. This work with all its contents, does not guarantee correctness, completion, quality or correctness of the provided information. Misinformation or misprints cannot be completely eliminated.

Printed in Great Britain
by Amazon